I Can Cook!

ITALIAN FOOD

Wendy Blaxland

A+

Smart Apple Media
P.O. Box 3263
Mankato, MN, 56002

First published in 2011 by
MACMILLAN EDUCATION AUSTRALIA PTY LTD
15–19 Claremont St, South Yarra, Australia 3141

Visit our website at www.macmillan.com.au or go directly to www.macmillanlibrary.com.au

Associated companies and representatives throughout the world.

Copyright text © Wendy Blaxland 2011

Library of Congress Cataloging-in-Publication Data

Blaxland, Wendy.
    Italian food / Wendy Blaxland.
        p. cm. — (I can cook!)
    Includes index.
    Summary:"Describes historical, cultural, and geographical factors that have influenced the cuisine of Italy.
    Includes recipes to create Italian food"—Provided by publisher.
    ISBN 978-1-59920-670-7 (library binding)
    1. Cooking, Italian—Juvenile literature. 2. Food—Italy—History—Juvenile literature. 3. Cookbooks. I. Title.
    TX723.B155 2012
641.5945—dc22
                            2011005446

Publisher: Carmel Heron
Commissioning Editor: Niki Horin
Managing Editor: Vanessa Lanaway
Editor: Laura Jeanne Gobal
Proofreaders: Georgina Garner; Kirstie Innes–Will
Designer: Stella Vassiliou
Page Layout: Stella Vassiliou
Photo Researcher: Claire Armstrong (management: Debbie Gallagher)
Illustrators: Jacki Sosenko; Guy Holt (map, **7**, **9**); Gregory Baldwin (map icons, **9**)
Production Controller: Vanessa Johnson

Manufactured in China by Macmillan Production (Asia) Ltd.
Kwun Tong, Kowloon, Hong Kong
Supplier Code: CP March 2011

Acknowledgments
The author would like to thank the following for their generous help and expert advice: Emeritus Professor Eugene Anderson, University of California; Lynne Olver, editor, FoodTimeline; Dena Saulsbury-Monaco, cook and librarian, Montreal; and Hiroko Tanaka, Venezia Marketing & Eventi.

The author and the publisher are grateful to the following for permission to reproduce copyright material:

Front cover photographs: Proscuitto and melon courtesy of iStockphoto.com/trutenka; mushroom risotto courtesy of Shutterstock/carlosdelacalle; margherita pizza courtesy of Shutterstock/Nayashkova Olga; spaghetti courtesy of Shutterstock/Andrea Skjold; berry granita courtesy of Shutterstock/Dusan Zidar. Back cover photographs: Brown paper bag courtesy of Shutterstock/Nils Z; chocolate salami courtesy of Shutterstock/ale1969; foccacia courtesy of Shutterstock/Michele Cozzolino; broccoli courtesy of Shutterstock/fotografaw; tomatoes courtesy of Shutterstock/Vitaly Korovin; basil courtesy of Shutterstock/Olga Miltsova; and zucchinis courtesy of Shutterstock/Anna Sedneva.

Photographs courtesy of: Dreamstime/Rnl, **30** (top); Getty Images/Thomas Barwick, **21** (risotto), /Dorota & Bogdan Bialy, **15** (bruschetta), /Food Photography Eising, **7** (top right), /Louise Lister, **25** (granita), /Kate Whitaker, **27** (pizza); iStockphoto.com/ajafoto, **10** (tea towel), /albertc111, **6** (travel stamps), /brinkstock, **13** (clipboard), /gbh007, **4** (girl), /gerisima, **6** (suitcase), /Irochka_T, **25** (ice), /Robyn Mac, **10** (hanging utensils), /Urosh Petrovic, **throughout** (red oven mitt); Photolibrary/Alamy/© foodfolio, **6** (pane carasau), /Alamy/© National Geographic Image Collection, **5** (bottom right), /Mario Matassa, **29** (bottom right), /MIXA Co Ltd, **19** (top left); PixMac/Orlando Bellini, **6** (pane di Altamura), /Comugnero Silvana, **7** (top left), **29** (top, bottom left), /wilderness, **7** (bottom); Shutterstock/ale1969, **23** (chocolate salami), /Aaron Amat, **11** (grater), /Ambrophoto, **8** (oranges), /Mark Aplet, **13** (electric mixer), /Aga & Miko Arsat, **8** (cod), /Hamiza Bakirci, **8** (strawberries), /barbaradudzinska, **17** (top left), /Roxana Bashyrova, **8** (grapes), /bgfreestyler, **16** (limes), **17** (limes), /Nikola Bilic, **9** (figs), /bonchan, **24** (raspberries), **25** (raspberries), /Adrian Britton, **10** (baking tray), /Darren Brode, **11** (electric mixer), /Sandra Caldwell, **27** (mozzarella), /Cameramannz, **8** (lamb chops), /Ilker Canikligil, **13** (saucepan), **31** (saucepan), /ZH Chen, **10** (measuring cups), /Coprid, **13** (soap dispenser), /Michele Cozzolino, **8** (foccacia), /Mikael Damkier, **10** (frying pan, measuring jug), /Raphael Daniaud, **11** (blender), /DanieleDM, **19** (spaghetti fork), /Le Do, **21** (spinach), /Ramon Grosso Dolarea, **7** (centre left), /Drozdowski , **16** (whole canteloupe), **17** (whole canteloupe), /Jaimie Duplass, **9** (rice), /Igor Dutina, **8** (proscuitto), /ejwhite, **11** (colander), /elenadesign, **8** (rice), /Elena Elisseeva, **8** (herbs, parmesan), **19** (herbs), /Christopher Elwell, **4** (ice cream cones), **5** (ice cream cone), /EtiAmmos, **4** (ice cream scoops), **5** (ice cream scoops), /Evitta, **28** (left), /Iakov Filimonov, **13** (knives), /BW Folsom, **8** (oval bread), /fotografaw, **8** (broccoli), /Gilmanshin, **13** (knife block), /grublee, **14** (tomatoes), **15** (tomatoes), **19** (tomatoes), /Hal_P, **9** (capsicums), /Jiang Hongyan, **22** (egg), **23** (eggs), /irin-k, **9** (sunflower), /Tischenko Irina, **10** (large knife, butter knife), /Eric Isselée, **9** (cow, sheep), /Ivaylo Ivanov, **8** (mushrooms), **21** (whole mushrooms), /K13 ART, **8** (blue bowl), **11** (bowls), /Kayros Studio, **13** (fire extinguisher), /Kira-N, **8** (potatoes), /Timo Kohlbacher, **22** (cocoa powder), **23** (cocoa powder), /Vitaly Korovin, **8** (tomatoes), /kosam, **8** (pasta), /Wolfe Larry, **26** (tomatoes), **27** (tomatoes), /LazarevDN, **8** (sieve), /Chris Leachman, **10** (chopping board), /Rudchenko Liliia, **8** (beef), /Svetlana Lukienko, **30** (bottom), /Lusoimages, **23** (biscuit), /Petr Malyshev, **13** (kettle), /Marco Mayer, **26** (top right), /Iain McGillivray, **10** (tongs), /Olga Miltsova, **15** (basil), /Luca Moi, **28** (right), /Mopic, **13** (first-aid box), /Lisovskaya Natalia, **8** (mozzarella), /Nattika, **8** (eggplants), /Nic Neish, **9** (prawns), /Nika Novak, **8** (cornmeal), /Olinchuk, **8** (seafood), /AntonioV Oquias, **16** (canteloupe slices), **17** (canteloupe slices), /ostromec, **8** (figs), /PashOK, **8** (cauliflower), /Isabella Pfenninger, **30** (middle), /photo-oasis, **8** (pork), /picturepartners, **9** (anchovies), /Tatiana Popova, **8** (watermelon), /Ragnarock, **11** (slotted spoon), **13** (frying pan), /ravl, **8** (cherries), /Stephen Aaron Rees, **11** (wooden spoon), /restyler, **8** (garlic), /Elena Schweitzer, **8** (pears), **9** (pears), /Anna Sedneva, **8** (zucchinis), /Helen Shorey, **21** (sliced mushrooms), /Maksymilian Skolik, **9** (hazelnuts), /soncerina, **10** (fork), /spe, **6** (grissini), /STILLFX, **10** (peeler), /Ev Thomas, **13** (fire blanket), /Matt Valentine, **10** (bread knife), /GraÃ§a Victoria, **10** (oven mitts), **10** (oven mitts), /Viktor1, **8** (sausages), /Vlue, **10** (steak knife), /Valentyn Volkov, **8** (artichokes, chestnuts, lemons, truffles), /Halina Yakushevich, **8** (apples), /Yonin, **9** (olives), /Peter Zijlstra, **8** (cabbage).

Contents

Glossary Words

When a word is printed in **bold**, it is explained in the Glossary on page 31.

Cooking Tips

Safety Warning

Ask an adult for help when you see this red oven mitt on a recipe.

How To

Cooking techniques are explained in small boxes with this handprint.

Some of the events in this book happened a long time ago, more than 2,000 years ago. To understand this, people measure time in years Before the Common Era (BCE) and during the Common Era (CE). It looks like this on a timeline.

| 150 | 100 | 50 | 0 | 50 | 100 | 150 |

Years BCE   Years CE

I Can Cook!

Cooking is a rewarding and lifelong skill. With some basic cooking knowledge, a little practice, and great recipes, you can cook entire meals! Cooking for your family and friends is a fun activity, and a mouthwatering meal can take you to places that you have never been. Are you ready to have fun cooking—and eating?

A World of Food

Every day, people all over the world cook delicious and **nutritious** meals. What they cook depends not only on the ingredients available to them, but also on their country's food **culture** or cooking style. A country's style of cooking is shaped over time by its culture, **economy**, **climate**, and the land itself.

Cook Your Way Around the World

You can explore the great cuisines of the world in your own kitchen. The special flavors and wonderful aromas of a country's food culture come from fresh ingredients and particular spices or herbs, which you can find in your local supermarket or a specialty store. Share with your family and friends authentic dishes from different countries that look great and taste even better.

You can cook mouthwatering food from different countries by following a few simple steps. Some recipes involve combining just a couple of ingredients!

Italian Food

Italian food is famous for its hearty nature, distinctive flavors and aromas, and rich colors. It is also easy and fun to cook.

Crowd-pleasing Cooking

Italian pizza, gelato, and pasta are loved all over the world. These foods and others developed as a result of Italy's unique history and landscape. Isolated city-states and even villages developed their own recipes for regional dishes based on simple but delicious ingredients found locally.

Cooking Italian Food at Home

You'll be surprised at how easy it is to cook an authentic Italian meal at home. This book has seven recipes that you can follow to cook a meal on your own or with a little help from an adult. Some of the recipes don't even involve cooking! The recipes can be adapted to suit special **diets**, too.

Italian Food Worldwide

Italian recipes have traveled around the world with **migrating** Italians, beginning in the 1800s CE. These days, it is easy to find lasagna in London and gnocchi in Brazil. In the United States (U.S.), pizza comes in at least three different forms—deep-dish in Chicago, thin in New York, and square-cut in St. Louis!

NORTH AMERICA

ITALY EUROPE ASIA

AFRICA

SOUTH AMERICA

AUSTRALIA

N

Mainland Italy is a boot-shaped peninsula located in southern Europe.

Gelato, Italy's version of ice cream, is a favorite treat of many children.

Traditions and Styles

For many hundreds of years, Italy was a divided land ruled by various groups of people. These people introduced their cooking **traditions** and styles to different areas of Italy and, though they may now be long gone, their influence can still be seen in Italian cooking today.

Different traditions have influenced the many types of Italian breads today, such as *pane di Altamura* (left) from Apulia, *grissini* (center) from Piedmont, and *pane carasau* (right) from the island of Sardinia.

Early Cultures

Italian cooking is rooted in the ancient Etruscan culture (700–100 BCE), from which focaccia and perhaps pasta originated. The huge, long-lasting Roman Empire (400 BCE–400 CE) brought to Italy baking skills from Greece and foreign ingredients, such as Egyptian watermelon.

Later Influences

From 900 CE, Arabs from Syria and North Africa brought with them lemons, spinach, coffee, rice, and couscous. The great trading city-state of Venice brought in spices and sugar from Asia, which were used to flavor Italian desserts. In the 1500s CE, important ingredients arrived from North and South America. Today, it is hard to imagine Italian cooking without tomatoes for pizza, corn for polenta, and chocolate for desserts. Migrants from former Italian **colonies** in North Africa have added their own flavors, too.

Pasta did not develop from noodles that the famous explorer Marco Polo brought back from China! Its likeliest influences are the dried noodles Arabs brought as a **staple food** when they invaded Sicily in the 900s CE.

Regional Food

From the wheat- and dairy-based cooking of the north to the fragrant tomato-and-olive-oil-based cooking of the south, every Italian region offers something different! The map below breaks Italy up into four main regions and discusses the ingredients and special foods that are popular in each.

North

Polenta (corn meal) is traditionally served with many dishes. Valle d'Aosta and Lombardy are famous for cheeses, such as gorgonzola and bel paese, while truffles, a fungus highly prized by **chefs** and food-lovers, grow in the forests of Piedmont. Focaccia is a Ligurian speciality and fish such as trout come from the region's lakes and the waters off the northern coasts. Venice and its surrounding areas are famous for seafood and vegetable risottos (pictured).

South

Southern Italian cooking includes simple dishes traditionally eaten by the poor, such as *pasta e fagioli* (pasta with beans, pictured) and rich, extravagant food, such as *zeppola*, a doughnut from Apulia. Sheep provide the main meat here, but seafood is also popular. Summer vegetables include tomatoes and eggplants. Onion and garlic are popular flavorings.

Central

This mountainous region is known for its fine Parma ham and Umbrian salami. Tuscany offers simple food based on bread, cheese, beans, fresh vegetables, and fruit. Emilia–Romagna boasts stuffed pasta dishes, including ravioli and tortellini (pictured), as well as lasagna.

Islands

Sicily was often invaded by Arab sailors, who introduced spices such as nutmeg, cinnamon, and cloves to the island's cuisine. Famous desserts include cassata (a sponge cake layered with ricotta cheese, candied peel, and a chocolate or vanilla filling, pictured) and granita (a semi-frozen treat). Seafood, such as lobster, squid, and tuna, is popular in Sardinia.

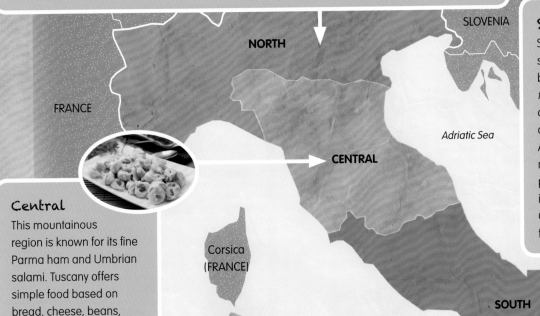

SLOVENIA

NORTH

FRANCE

CENTRAL

Adriatic Sea

Corsica (FRANCE)

Tyrrhenian Sea

SOUTH

ISLANDS
Sardinia

ISLANDS
Sicily

Italian Ingredients

Italian ingredients vary, from the meat, fish, cheese, and egg-based pasta of northern and central Italy, to the tomato-based sauces of the south, served over dried pasta and flavored with olives and garlic. However, the one thing Italian cooking styles have in common is the use of fresh, seasonal produce.

Meat
Italians cook with beef, pork, and lamb, and also love sausages and ham.

Seafood
The waters off Italy's long coastline provide fine fish, from anchovies to sea bass, and other seafood, such as calamari and clams.

Dairy Products
Cheese features in many recipes. Italy has many distinctive cheeses, including pecorino and bocconcini.

Fruit
Fresh, seasonal fruit includes apples, pears, lemons, and oranges, along with grapes, watermelons, cherries, figs, and strawberries in summer.

Staple Foods
Bread and pasta made from wheat flour are staple foods in Italy. Rice is popular too. Corn-based polenta is a northern staple.

Vegetables
Tomatoes, zucchini, eggplants, broccoli, and cauliflower feature in southern cooking, while cabbage and potatoes are popular in the north. Mushrooms, truffles, garlic, and herbs, such as basil, rosemary, oregano, and thyme, are used for flavor.

Landscapes and Climates

The varied Italian landscapes and climates produce different ingredients in different regions. Mountains separate Italy from the rest of Europe along its northern border and also run north to south down the middle of the country. Italy's landscapes include **fertile** valleys, forests, long coastlines, and dry plains, all with their own produce. The map below shows which areas of the country Italy's produce comes from.

Chestnuts and hazelnuts, grown especially for sweet treats such as hazelnut spreads, come from the north.

Farmers grow corn in the north. Rice is grown along the Po Valley in northern Lombardy and in the Piedmont and Veneto area.

AUSTRIA

SLOVENIA

NORTH

Farmers raise cattle for beef and dairy products in the north and center. Pigs are also raised in the north and goats in mountainous areas.

Adriatic Sea

CENTRAL

Rapeseed, from which canola oil is made, and sunflowers for oil are grown on the inland plains in the north and central regions.

In the cooler climate of the north, potatoes, cabbage, apples, and pears are grown. The fertile Po Valley produces asparagus and fruit such as cherries, peaches, nectarines, grapes, figs, and berries.

Corsica (FRANCE)

SOUTH

Sheep are farmed mainly in the south.

Tyrrhenian Sea

ISLANDS Sardinia

Melons, grapes, and citrus fruit, such as lemons and oranges, are farmed in the warmer south, as well as tomatoes, artichokes, bell peppers, eggplant, onions, and garlic.

The waters off the long coastline provide seafood, including cod, anchovies, and shrimp.

ISLANDS Sicily

Durum wheat for dried pasta is grown in the river valleys and in the south. Buckwheat and farro are also grown here, along with olives.

9

Equipment

Having the right equipment to cook with is very important. Here are some of the most common items needed in the kitchen.

Potato mashers break up food.

Frying pans fry or brown food.

Sieves separate and break up food.

Spatulas lift and turn food.

Cook pasta, rice, soups, and stews in saucepans.

Big knives chop. Small knives cut and peel. Butter knives spread. Serrated knives slice.

Oven mitts protect hands from heat.

Baking pans hold food in an oven.

Peelers remove the skins from fruit and vegetables.

Forks hold, stir, or prick food.

Whisks beat food to add air and make it light.

Tongs are used to handle hot food.

Measuring cups and spoons measure ingredients accurately.

Cutting boards provide safe surfaces for cutting food.

Blenders chop ingredients, mix food, and make smooth sauces and soups.

Spoons mix and stir. Wooden spoons prevent scratched pans. Slotted spoons let liquid drain away.

Graters shave thin slices from food, such as cheese.

Colanders drain liquids.

Mixers mix food quickly.

Bowls hold food for mixing.

Cooking Basics

Weight, Volume, Temperature, and Special Diets

It is important to use the right amount of ingredients, cook at the correct heat, and be aware of people with special dietary needs.

Weight and Volume

The weight and volume of ingredients can be measured with a weighing scale or with measuring cups and spoons. Convert them using this table. Measure dry ingredients so that they are level across the top of the spoon or cup without packing them down.

Recipe Measurement		Weight	Volume
	1 cup	8 ounces	250 ml
	½ cup	4 ounces	125 ml
	2 tablespoons	1 ounce	30 ml
	1 teaspoon	0.16 ounce	4.7 ml

Temperature

Fahrenheit and Celsius are two different ways of measuring temperature. Oven dials may show the temperature in either Fahrenheit or Celsius. Use lower temperatures in gas or convection ovens.

Oven Temperature	Celsius	Fahrenheit
Slow	150°	300°
Moderately slow	160°–170°	320°–340°
Moderate	180°	350°
Moderately hot	190°	375°
Hot	200°	400°
Very hot	220°–240°	430°–470°

Special Diets

Some people follow special diets because of personal or religious beliefs about what they should eat. Others must not eat certain foods because they are **allergic** to them.

Diet	What It Means	Symbol
Allergy-specific	Some people's bodies react to a certain food as if it were poison. They may die from eating even a tiny amount of this food. Nuts, eggs, milk, strawberries, and even chocolate may cause allergic reactions.	
Halal	**Muslims** eat only food prepared according to strict religious guidelines. This is called halal food.	
Kosher	**Jews** eat only food prepared according to strict religious guidelines. This is called kosher food.	
Vegan	Vegans eat nothing from animals, including dairy products, eggs, and honey.	
Vegetarian	Vegetarians eat no animal products and may or may not eat dairy products, eggs, and honey.	

Safety and Hygiene

Be safe in the kitchen by staying alert and using equipment correctly when cooking. Practicing good food hygiene means you always serve clean, germ-free food. Follow the handy tips below!

Be Organized
Hungry? Organized cooks eat sooner! First, read the recipe. Next, take out the equipment and ingredients you'll need and follow the stages set out in the recipe. Straighten up and clean as you go. While your food cooks, wash up, sweep the kitchen floor, and empty the garbage.

Heat
Place boiling saucepans toward the back of the stove with handles turned inward. Keep your hands and face away from steam and switch hot equipment off as soon as you have finished using it. Use oven mitts to pick up hot pots and put them down on heatproof surfaces. Always check that food is cool enough to eat.

Emergencies
All kitchens should have a fire blanket, fire extinguisher, and first-aid box.

Food Hygiene
To avoid spreading germs, wash your hands well and keep coughs and sneezes away from food. Use fresh ingredients and always store food that spoils easily, such as meat and fish, in the refrigerator.

Electricity
Use electrical equipment only with an adult's help. Switch the power off before unplugging any equipment and keep it away from water.

Knives
When cutting food with a knife, cut away from yourself and onto a nonslip surface, such as a suitable cutting board.

13

Let's Cook!

MAKES: 2 slices

PREPARATION TIME: 5 minutes

COOKING TIME: 2 minutes

FOOD VALUES: About 135 **calories**, 5 grams of fat, 3 grams of **protein**, and 15 grams of **carbohydrates** per slice.

SPECIAL DIETS: Suitable for vegan, vegetarian, nut-free, dairy-free, kosher, and halal diets. For **gluten**-free diets, use gluten-free bread, rice cakes, or crackers.

Bruschetta

Some people say bruschetta developed in the 1400s CE in Tuscany, Umbria, and Lazio to promote the new season's olive oil through its use on lightly toasted bread. Others say bruschetta was a way of using up stale bread. A delicious appetizer, this bruschetta showcases good Italian wood-fired bread and really ripe tomatoes.

Equipment

- Small, sharp knife
- Cutting board
- Small bowl
- Wooden spoon
- Measuring spoon
- Toaster (or grill)
- Serving plate

Ingredients

- 1 large, ripe, full-flavored tomato, washed
- 1 teaspoon of olive oil
- A handful of basil leaves, washed
- 1 clove of garlic
- 2 thick slices of wood-fired Italian bread (or your favorite bread)

What to Do

1 Cut the core of the tomato carefully from its stem end and throw it away. Next, cut the tomato in half and dice it.

2 Place the diced tomato in the small bowl and mix it with the olive oil.

3 Cut the basil leaves into ribbons.

14

Recipe Variations

Add half of a diced red onion to the tomato and olive oil mixture.

Use slices of baguette, a French bread, to create mini-bruschetta for a party.

Ask an adult for help with using the knife and toaster or grill.

4 Halve the clove of garlic.

5 Toast the bread lightly in a toaster until it browns, then rub the cut face of the garlic across one side of the toasted bread.

6 Pile the diced tomato on the garlic-rubbed side of the toasted bread. Scatter the basil ribbons over the tomato and serve immediately.

15

Melon and Prosciutto Antipasto

Antipasto is the traditional first course of an Italian meal. It developed from the tradition of serving many dishes during large dinners for the rich, including small portions of different foods, such as olives, **cured meat**, and cheeses. In this antipasto recipe, the strong flavor of the prosciutto, a cured meat, contrasts with the sweet taste of the melon.

MAKES: 6 servings

PREPARATION TIME: 10 minutes

FOOD VALUES: About 75 calories, 3 g of fat, 5 g of protein, and 8 g of carbohydrates per serving.

SPECIAL DIETS: Suitable for nut-free and gluten-free diets. For vegan, vegetarian, kosher, and halal diets, use a sliced prune instead of prosciutto.

Equipment

- Tablespoon
- Cutting board
- Small, sharp knife
- Serving plate
- Fork and knife (or napkin)

Ingredients

- ½ of a cantaloupe
- ½ of a lime (or lemon)
- 6 slices of prosciutto

What to Do

1 Use the tablespoon to scoop out the seeds from the cantaloupe and throw them away.

2 Cut the cantaloupe into 6 crescent-shaped slices and arrange them in a circle or line on the plate.

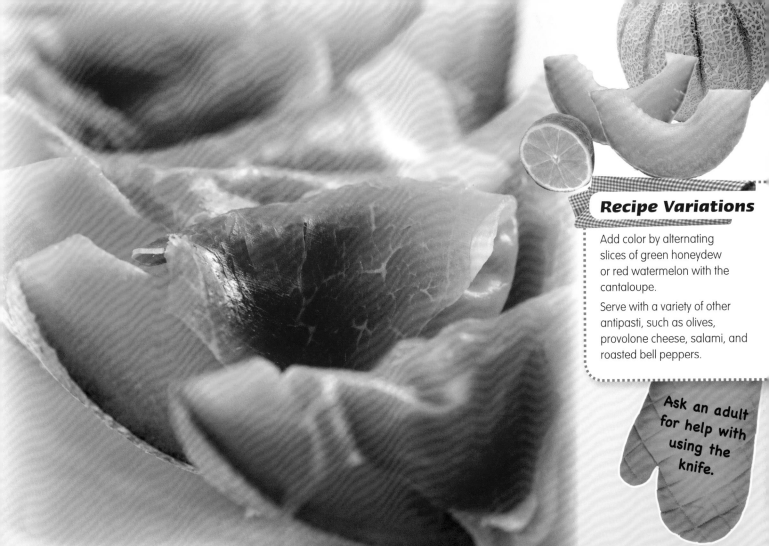

Ask an adult for help with using the knife.

Squeeze the lime juice over the cantaloupe slices.

Drape a slice of prosciutto elegantly over each slice of cantaloupe.

Serve with a fork and knife or just a napkin. Remember to provide a plate for the cantaloupe **rinds**.

Let's Cook!

Spaghetti Bolognese

This famous dish is probably better known outside Italy! The traditional bolognese meat sauce from Bologna includes very little tomato and goes better with flat pasta, such as lasagna or tagliatelle. This nontraditional recipe combines a thick, meat-flavored tomato sauce with spaghetti. Dig in!

MAKES: 4 servings

PREPARATION TIME: 10 minutes

COOKING TIME: 20 minutes

FOOD VALUES: About 280 calories, 7 g of fat, 18 g of protein, and 41 g of carbohydrates per serving.

SPECIAL DIETS: Suitable for nut-free diets. For vegan and vegetarian diets, replace the meat with crumbled tofu, mashed beans, or chickpeas; vegans should also avoid the cheese; for gluten-free diets use corn, buckwheat, or rice pasta; and for kosher and halal diets, leave out the bacon or pancetta and use certified minced beef.

Equipment

- Large frying pan
- Wooden spoon
- Large saucepan
- Colander
- Large serving bowl with tongs
- Small serving bowl with spoon

Ingredients

- 1 large onion, diced
- 2 cloves of garlic, chopped
- 1 teaspoon of olive oil (or other vegetable oil)
- 2 slices of lean bacon or pancetta (a cured meat), diced
- 4 tablespoons of fresh basil, oregano, rosemary, and thyme, chopped (or 2 tablespoons of dried Italian herbs)
- ½ pound of lean ground beef
- 1 package of dried spaghetti (or other pasta)
- ½ teaspoon of salt and extra to taste
- 6 ripe tomatoes, chopped (or 1 can of diced tomatoes)
- 1 cup of tomato paste
- A few fresh basil leaves
- Chunk of strong cheese (parmesan or cheddar), grated

What to Do

1 Cook the onion and garlic in oil in the frying pan until the onion turns transparent.

2 Add the bacon or pancetta and chopped herbs. Cook for 2–5 minutes, stirring.

3 Add the ground beef and cook until the meat turns brown (about 5–7 minutes).

How To: Test pasta

To test that pasta is cooked, use a fork and take one strand out of the saucepan after 10 minutes. Blow on the pasta to cool it, then bite it. If it resists just a little, the pasta is ready.

Recipe Variations

Try adding pesto (a basil and pine nut paste) or chopped celery and carrots to the sauce.

Use pasta in different shapes, such as *fusilli* (spirals), *orecchiette* (little ears), *conchiglie* (shells), or *farfalle* (butterflies).

Ask an adult for help with using the stove.

4 Fill the saucepan about ⅔ full with cold water, add half a teaspoon of salt, and bring the water to a boil on the stove. When it boils, add the spaghetti gently. **Test** a strand of spaghetti after 10 minutes. When it is cooked, drain the pasta in the colander and put it in the large serving bowl.

5 While the pasta is cooking, add the tomatoes and tomato paste to the meat, and cook on low to medium heat for about 10 minutes. Stir regularly to prevent the sauce from sticking to the pan. Add a little water if needed. Taste the sauce and add salt or more herbs if necessary.

6 Pour the sauce over the pasta in the serving bowl. **Garnish** with fresh basil and serve with the grated cheese in the small serving bowl.

19

Mushroom Risotto

Arabs brought rice to Sicily in the 900s CE, but it was not introduced in the Po Valley until the 1200s CE, probably by the Spanish. Risotto, an Italian rice dish, was invented in the 1500s CE. Unlike traditional rice dishes, which are dry, risotto is creamy because the rice is cooked in a large amount of stock that has been flavored with different ingredients.

MAKES: 4 servings

PREPARATION TIME: 10 minutes

COOKING TIME: oven—40 minutes; microwave—35 minutes

FOOD VALUES: About 370 calories, 10 g of fat, 22 g of protein, and 55 g of carbohydrates per serving.

SPECIAL DIETS: Suitable for vegetarian, nut-free, gluten-free, kosher, and halal diets. For vegan diets, use soy cheese instead of parmesan.

Equipment

- Tea kettle
- Measuring cup
- Ovenproof casserole dish with lid or large microwave-safe casserole dish with lid
- Oven mitts
- Wooden spoon

Ingredients

- 5 cups of water
- 2 cups of arborio rice (or other rice suitable for risotto)
- 1 tablespoon of butter (or margarine)
- 1 tablespoon of vegetable bouillon powder (or 3 cubes, crumbled)
- 1 cup of mushrooms, cut into small chunks
- 2 cups of baby spinach leaves
- 1 cup of grated hard cheese (try parmesan)

What to Do

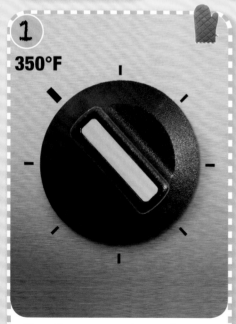

1

350°F

Turn the oven on to moderate heat (350°F), if you're not using the microwave.

2

Fill the tea kettle with 5 cups of water and boil.

3

Put the rice, butter, bouillon powder, mushrooms, and hot water in the casserole dish and cover.

Recipe Variations

Try a meat risotto with ¾ of a cup of Italian sausage chunks, ¾ of a cup of mushrooms, and fresh rosemary. Use a meat bouillon instead of vegetable bouillon.

Mold leftover risotto into small patties and roast them on a lightly oiled baking pan or heat them in sugo (an Italian-style tomato sauce).

Ask an adult for help with using the tea kettle and oven or microwave.

4 Put the casserole dish in the oven and bake for 40 minutes or place in the microwave and cook on high for 35 minutes, stopping it to stir once after 20 minutes. (If using the microwave, jump to step 6 next.)

5 After 35 minutes, take the casserole dish out of the oven, using a pair of oven mitts. If most of the liquid has been absorbed, it is ready. Otherwise, leave it in the oven for another 5 minutes.

6 Add the baby spinach leaves and grated cheese. Mix well and enjoy.

Chocolate Salami

This delicious dessert from Lombardy couldn't be easier to make. Its main ingredients are chocolate and cookies—and it has nothing to do with meat! Often, this may be the first recipe that Italian mothers teach their children because it needs no cooking. It is fun to make and fun to eat!

MAKES: 6 pieces

PREPARATION TIME: 15 minutes

SETTING TIME: 1½ hours in the refrigerator (or 30 minutes in the freezer)

FOOD VALUES: About 195 calories, 11 g of fat, 3 g of protein, and 50 g of carbohydrates per piece.

SPECIAL DIETS: Suitable for vegetarian and nut-free diets. For vegan diets, replace the egg with ⅓ of a cup of cooked apple or mashed banana; and for gluten-free, kosher, and halal diets, choose gluten-free or certified biscuits.

Equipment

- Mixing bowl
- Wooden spoon
- Cutting board
- 16 inches of parchment paper
- Sharp knife

Ingredients

- 1 egg
- 3½ ounces of butter (or margarine), roughly chopped
- 3½ ounces of sugar
- 5⅓ ounces of sweet cookies (try shortbread)
- 1¾ ounces of cocoa powder

What to Do

1 Break the egg into the mixing bowl.

2 Add the butter and sugar to the egg and mix until it looks creamy.

3 Break the cookies into pieces.

Recipe Variations

Replace the cocoa powder with 3½ ounces of melted dark cooking chocolate, the sugar with 1 tablespoon of treacle, and use just 1 ounce of butter. When the chocolate salami has hardened, dust its surface with icing sugar.

Add 1 cup of chopped dried fruit and nuts to the salami mixture for a different taste and texture.

Ask an adult for help with using the knife.

4

Add the cookie pieces and cocoa powder to the butter, sugar, and egg mixture. Mix thoroughly.

5

Transfer the mixture onto the parchment paper and mold it into a salami-like shape. Wrap the parchment paper around the chocolate salami.

6

Chill the chocolate salami in the refrigerator for 1½ hours or in the freezer for 30 minutes until it hardens. Slice the chocolate salami, remove the parchment paper, then arrange the slices on a plate and serve.

Let's Cook!

Raspberry Granita

Ice has been used for thousands of years to cool drinks. The early Romans used snow from Mount Etna for just this purpose. Frozen, fruit-based treats, such as sorbet and granita, developed along with ice cream in the second half of the 1600s CE. Granita is a semi-frozen dessert from the island of Sicily, where it is often served for breakfast with a brioche (sweet bun).

Equipment

- 2 medium-size bowls
- Fork
- Sieve
- Spatula
- Wide, shallow freezer-safe container
- Small saucepan
- Measuring cup
- Wooden spoon
- Tablespoon
- 2 tall glasses, chilled

Ingredients

- 4 cups of fresh (or thawed frozen) raspberries
- ¼ cup of white sugar
- 1 cup of water

What to Do

1 Set aside a few raspberries to use as a garnish. Mash the remaining raspberries with a fork.

2 Press the mashed raspberries through the sieve with the spatula. Throw away the seeds. Transfer the raspberry purée to the freezer-safe container.

3 Place the sugar and water in the saucepan and stir over low heat for a few minutes until the sugar dissolves.

24

Recipe Variations

Try other fruit, such as strawberries or lemons, instead.

Add a few fresh leaves of mint or grate some lemon zest and mix it into the granita for a new flavor.

Ask an adult for help with using the stove.

4

Pour the sugar and water mixture into the raspberry purée and stir well.

5

Freeze the raspberry mixture for 20–30 minutes. Take the container out of the freezer. Scrape the crystals from the sides of the container with the tablespoon and mix them through the granita. Put the container back in the freezer. Repeat this step until the granita is almost fully frozen (about 1½ hours).

6

Scrape the granita into the chilled glasses with the tablespoon. Garnish with whole raspberries and serve.

Let's Cook!

Pizza Margherita

The ancient Greeks, who occupied southern Italy between 730 and 130 BCE, made a very early version of pizza by topping dough with herbs, vegetables, or cheese. Italian cooks began to use South American tomatoes widely only during the 1700s and 1800s CE. Pizza margherita was invented in Naples by chef Raffaele Esposito in 1889 CE to honor Italy's Queen Margherita. This pizza bears the three colors of the Italian flag: red (tomatoes), white (mozzarella), and green (basil).

Equipment

- 2 baking pans
- Bowl
- Wooden spoon
- Oven mitts

Ingredients

- 1 teaspoon of olive oil
- 2 ready-made pizza crusts

TOMATO SAUCE

- 2 cloves of garlic, chopped
- Handful of fresh basil leaves, chopped
- 1 cup of crushed tomatoes

TOPPING

- Handful of grated or shaved parmesan
- 4½-ounce ball of mozzarella, sliced
- Handful of cherry tomatoes, halved
- Handful of fresh basil leaves

What to Do

1

480°F

Turn the oven on to 480°F.

2

Oil the baking pans with the olive oil and put the pizza crusts on the pans.

3

Make the sauce by mixing the garlic and chopped basil with the crushed tomatoes.

Try another traditional Italian pizza topping, using 4 sprigs of fresh or 2 teaspoons of dried oregano, 6 chopped anchovies, and 2 chopped cloves of garlic.

Use meat or vegetables to create a gourmet pizza with your own special combination of flavors.

Ask an adult for help with using the oven.

4

Smooth the sauce over the pizza crusts with the back of the wooden spoon.

5

Sprinkle the parmesan and place the mozzarella and cherry tomatoes on top of the sauce.

6

Bake the pizzas in the oven for 8–10 minutes or until crisp. Remove the baking pans from the oven with a pair of oven mitts. Set them on a heatproof surface and sprinkle the fresh basil leaves on top. Serve immediately.

An Italian Food Celebration: Carnevale di Venezia

Carnevale di Venezia, or the Carnival of Venice, is an annual festival celebrated in the northern Italian city of Venice. People from around the world come to this city to join the Italians for two weeks of **mischief** and fun!

What Is Carnevale?

Carnevale is a festival that began in the 1500s CE as a period of celebration without the normal social rules. It was and still is the custom to dress up and wear masks that hide a person's identity. Carnevale is celebrated for two weeks and ends the day before the **Catholic** holy day of Ash Wednesday. Though the Carnevale di Venezia is the most well-known, similar carnivals are celebrated all over Italy.

How Is Carnevale Celebrated?

In Venice, visitors join locals in wearing extravagant clothes and masks that are often based on Italian theater masks. While disguised, people have fun at masquerade balls and on the streets. The saying is, "anything goes at Carnevale," and pranks are all part of the fun! Different Italian cities have their own traditions and special foods. The town of Viareggio holds parades with spectacular floats made from papier-mâché.

Masks are available for sale in Venice all year round, not just during Carnevale.

Revelers in Venice enjoy designing their Carnevale costumes and showing them off.

Food

Sweet treats prepared just for Carnevale include the traditional pastries *cenci* (fried pastry), *frittelle* (fritters), and *spirali alla Grappa* (funnel-shaped pastry with raspberry sauce). Savory and sweet *tortelli* (stuffed pasta) stem from pastries made by street food sellers thousands of years ago during the original Roman religious celebrations from which Carnevale began. The same can be said for the rich *lasagna di Carnevale*.

Carnevale

The Italian word "carnevale" comes from the term "carne levare," which means "remove the meat." It refers to the Catholic custom of not eating meat during Lent, the period of time before Carnevale, as an offering to God.

These sweet pastries are made specially for carnivals around Italy. Different names are used for them in various regions.

Try This!

Cooking is a creative skill you can enjoy every day. Try these activities and learn more about cooking Italian food.

- Ask an adult to take you to a *gelataria* (Italian ice-cream shop) on your birthday. What is your favorite flavor of gelato?

- Visit your local library and borrow some Italian cookbooks. What is the most unusual Italian recipe you can find? Can you make it?

- Plant an Italian herb garden with parsley, oregano, rosemary, thyme, and basil. Find out which herbs are perennials (growing for two years or more) and which ones need to be replanted each year.

- Celebrate an Italian holiday by making a red, white, and green fruit salad with strawberries or watermelon balls, green grapes, and chunks of apple sprinkled with lemon juice.

- Start a mini-Mediterranean vegetable garden with cherry tomatoes, baby eggplants, zucchini, and bell peppers. How many Italian recipes can you find that use these ingredients?

- Learn the names of all the food mentioned in this book in Italian and use them the next time you're in an Italian restaurant.

- Find an Italian recipe that uses a vegetable or fruit that is new to you. Try it!

- There are many different pasta shapes. How many can you find and what do their names mean?

Glossary

allergic
having an allergy, or a bad reaction to certain foods

calories
units measuring the amount of energy food provides

carbohydrates
substances that provide the body with energy

Catholic
relating to the religion of Catholicism

chefs
skilled and trained cooks

climate
the general weather conditions of an area

colonies
countries or areas controlled by another country

culture
the ways of living that a group of people has developed over time

cured meat
meat that has been preserved or flavored through a process such as salting or smoking

diets
foods and drinks normally consumed by different people or groups of people

economy
the system of trade by which a country makes and uses its wealth

fertile
capable of producing good crops

garnish
use a small amount of a certain food to add flavor or color to a dish

gluten
a protein found in wheat and some other grains that makes dough springy

Jews
people who follow the religion of Judaism

migrating
moving from one country to another to live permanently

mischief
slightly bad, but not harmful or damaging, behavior

Muslims
people who follow the religion of Islam

nutritious
providing nutrients, or nourishment

protein
a nutrient that helps bodies grow and heal

rinds
the thick, firm outer layers or coverings of certain fruit and food

staple food
a food that is eaten regularly and is one of the main parts of a diet

traditions
patterns of behavior handed down through generations

Index